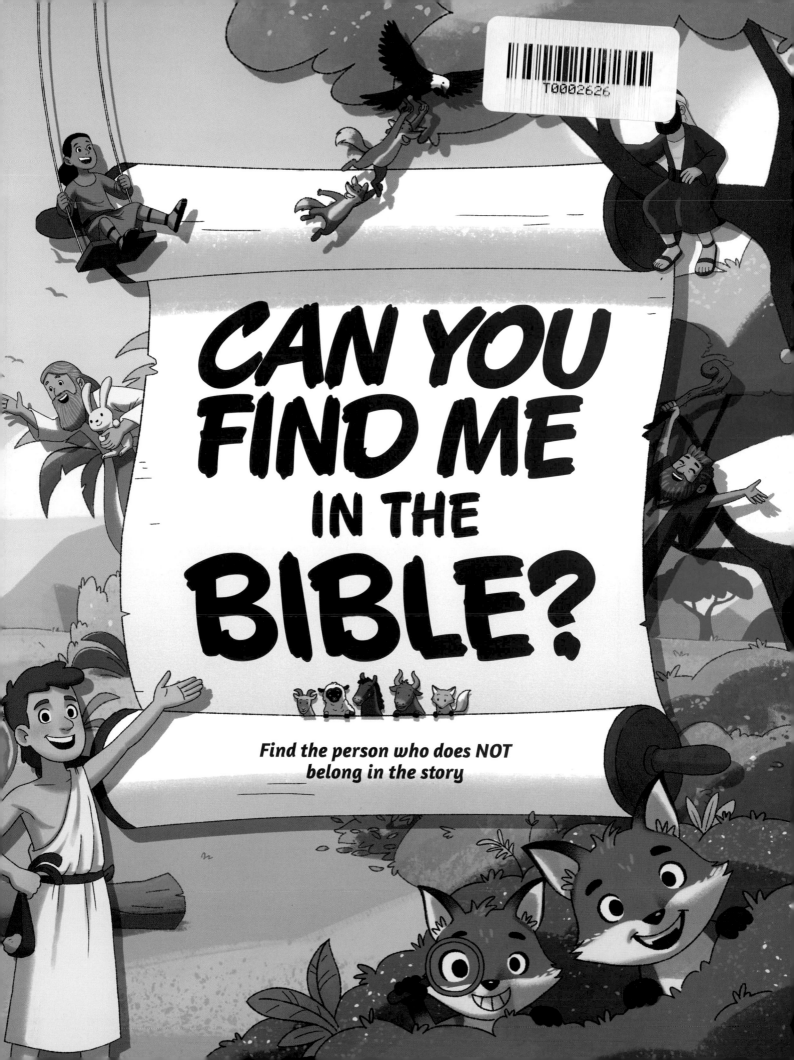

CAN YOU FIND ME IN THE BIBLE?

Find the person who does NOT belong in the story

HOW TO PLAY

Well, this is strange...Not only am I wet and smelly, but I'm also in the wrong story. Many of my other Bible friends in this book are too.

My name is Jonah, by the way. Nice to meet you.

Can you find the person who does not belong in the story? While you're at it, find the other things in each scene, too.

Then we can figure out where we belong. Thanks, you're the best!

Can You Find Me in the Bible?

Published by Kregel Children's, an imprint of Kregel Publications, 2450 Oak Industrial Dr. NE, Grand Rapids, MI 49505, USA.

Original edition published in Denmark under the title *Can You Find Me in the Bible?* by Scandinavia Publishing House, Copenhagen, Denmark. Copyright © 2023 Scandinavia Publishing House. All rights reserved.

Text by Andrew Newton
Illustrations by Mario Gushiken
Cover design and Layout by Gao Hanyu

ISBN 978-0-8254-4848-5

Printed in China

CONTENTS

CREATION

Hey, I'm David! Wow, look at this garden. It's so beautiful! There's trees and plants with delicious fruit, and the animals are all playing together, even the rabbit and the turtle! It's so different from the field where I watch my sheep. See? They must be Adam and Eve, the first people God created. Everything God made in the garden of Eden is very good!

Find me and my sheep!

Also find:

NOAH'S ARK

Hi, I am Daniel. That's the biggest boat I've ever seen! I wonder where it's going to float. I don't see any water nearby. There are so many animals, too! There's two of each, and they're all heading to the boat. Oh, here are the lions. I love them. I once spent a whole night in a den full of lions.

Find me and my furry friend!

Also find:

MOSES AT THE RED SEA

Hey, I'm Adam! Look at that, Eve! The water is parting, and all those people are walking through on dry land. The fish look so confused! That man with the staff looks like he's praying. God must be helping the people escape through the sea. Even though we're not in our garden, God is still in control of His creation.

Find us among the people!

Also find:

DAVID AND GOLIATH

Hi, I'm Zacchaeus! Oh my, how did I end up on this battlefield so far from my tax booth? That giant must be the Philistines' champion. If I stay in this tree, I will be as tall as he is. But wait! That's just a little shepherd boy going out to fight him. He doesn't have any armor on, and his only weapon is a sling and some stones. He must really trust God!

Find me cheering for David!

Also find:

Hello, I'm baby Jesus! I know that angel! He's one of the ones that sang for the shepherds on my birthday. But wait, is that Daniel? This must be the den of lions where the king had to put Daniel after his advisors tricked him. I'm so glad my Father looks out for people who love Him. Those lions aren't even trying to bite Daniel.

Find Me in the lions' den!

15

Also find:

Hey there, I'm Peter! Wow, that was some storm. It reminds me of the time Jesus came walking out on the water to see us. I wonder who the sailors threw overboard? He probably wishes he could walk on water right now! That big fish is going to swallow him. That must be Jonah! Does God still have a big plan for him?

Find me here at sea!

Also find:

Hi, I'm the boy with bread and fish! Those guys look rich and important. I wonder what they're doing in a place like this with all these animals. Everyone is looking at that young woman and her baby. Was He born in this stable? They even brought gifts for Him! I wonder if they would like to share my lunch.

Find me here at Jesus' birth!

19

Also find:

Hello there, I'm Samson! Did you see that? I saw that servant put water in the jar, but now that he's serving it, it turned into wine—a miracle! I wonder who that man is talking to the servants? I wish He'd been at my wedding. My wedding was attended by a bunch of angry Philistines who were jealous of my incredible strength.

Find me fighting a lion!

21

Also find:

THE FEEDING OF THE 5,000

Hi, I'm Joseph! This hillside is a nice change from the Egyptian desert. It's just as crowded as when everyone came to buy food from me! Did all these people come to hear that man teach? He's passing around some food that boy gave him. It looked like there were just two fish and five loaves of bread, but everyone has plenty to eat.

Find me in my red coat!

23

Also find:

Hello, I'm Noah! Oh my, this is a lot of kids. I wonder if these people are their parents. They're all gathering around that man. He seems so kind. He is making time for all of them, even though His friends don't seem to want all these children around. I heard someone say He's a carpenter. Maybe He can help me with my boat.

Find me and my cute bunnies!

25

Also find:

ZACCHAEUS MEETS JESUS

Greetings to you, I'm Moses! There sure is a big crowd over there. I wonder who that person in the tree is. Perhaps he had trouble seeing over the crowd. Maybe I could part the crowd with my staff like God parted the sea for me. Oh, the person named Jesus is talking to the man in the tree. He looks so happy!

Find me in the crowd!

27

Also find:

It's me, Jonah, again! It's so nice to be back in Jerusalem. It's way better than inside the belly of that fish! I wonder who all these people are? That man over there is talking about someone named Jesus, and those people are giving up things they don't need to help others. Everywhere I look, I can see God's love in action.

Find me among these first followers of Jesus!

Before I go, here's an **Extra Challenge:**

#1 Find the guy with 2 different outfits.

#2 Which 2 guys only show up once?

29

Also find:

ANSWER KEY

Read more about the **Creation** of the world in the Bible in Genesis 1-4 and **David** in 1 Samuel 17.

Read about **Noah's Ark** in Genesis 6 and **Daniel** in Daniel 6.

Read about **Moses at the Red Sea** in Exodus 13-14 and **Adam and Eve** in Genesis 1.

Read about **David and Goliath** in 1 Samuel 17 and **Zacchaeus** in Luke 19.

Read about **Daniel and the Lions** in Daniel 6 and **The Birth of Baby Jesus** in Luke 2.

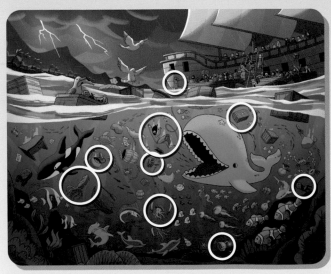

Read about **Jonah and the Big Fish** in Jonah 1-4 and **Peter Walking on Water** in Matthew 14:22-33.